A Beginners Gui[de] Use Social Media for Profit

Table of Contents

Introduction

I want to thank you and congratulate you for purchasing the book "A Beginners Guide to Use Social Media for Profit."

We live in a world where we are becoming increasingly social – even if human interaction is not such a big thing as it used to be before the existence of social media. True, social media has completely revolutionized the way we interact with each other and even in how we run our businesses. If you are looking to take those profits of yours to an unprecedented level as far as your business is concerned, you simply have to be on those social media platforms. The thing is, simply *being on them* is not enough. You have to make your presence felt in such a way that people in the digital avenues out there actually see you screaming from the rooftops. Yes, you need to ensure that whatever you say out there on those platforms out there – is heard...

With the vast amount of social media content out there, you must be wondering exactly how your brand is going to be noticed. In fact, you might even be thinking how any single brand gets noticed at all, right? Well, the answer is simple. You can indeed be noticed far more than the several thousands of others desperately vying to get noticed where it comes to that common target audience, if you employ the right strategies that are discussed in this book. *What strategies?* You might ask. Well then, it's about time we begin!

Chapter 1: Facebook

Facebook is by and large the largest social media platform out there, and it would be impossible to get anywhere in your online business journey without hopping onto the Facebook bandwagon. Let's take a look at exactly what the best strategies are, where it comes to employing Facebook to market our brand!

Strategies to leverage your brand worth on Facebook

Find out the best time to post.

Facebook has a really great tool called *Facebook Insights*. You can use this tool to find out when is the average time that your fan base is online, and accordingly post that content of yours. This will help ensure that the content you post has a far greater chance of actually being seen out there!

Be more human.

Facebook is really not all that a professional site, and it would help to keep in tandem with the essence of the site by infusing a lot of entertaining and even inspirational posts every now and then. This will help to ensure that the content you post is forever fresh and entertaining, and also deepen the very real human bond between the people that like your page and you.

Use videos.

Of late there is a vast number of people who are turning to watch videos on Facebook, be they entertainment or business related. You should ensure that you capitalize on this fact and create some really great videos that you can post every now and then, pertaining to your company or brand.

Use photos.

Nothing quite says something like a picture does. When you are posting status updates, you might wish to accompany them every now and then with a really well taken picture. That will serve to drive engagement with that particular post considerably.

Post at non-peak times as well.

Yes, you heard it right. You want to post at the right times as we have discussed, but you might want to post that content at non-peak times as well. This is when there is far less overall traffic and your post will thus have far greater chances of being discovered in the process.

Schedule your status updates.

This is one of the best possible ways to ensure that you never forget top post great content. For instance, if you have several ideas now you might wish to create related posts now and then schedule them to appear later. In this way you forever remain consistent where it comes to posting regular content, and you also make sure you never miss a really great idea when you get one.

Chapter 2: Twitter

Have something you want to Tweet about? Well, make sure you do it just right with these powerful strategies that will help you gain that edge on this all-important social media platform.

Strategies to leverage your brand worth on Twitter

Use those keywords in your tweets.

One of the best possible ways to actually get that content of yours noticed out there on social media, is to use keywords effectively. You will find that when you use those keywords in your tweets, your tweets have a far larger chance of being noticed. Make sure you use those tweets that are most closely related to your industry, of course.

Increase the number of clicks and retweets using images.

Like in Facebook, you want to use images to increase the chances of those retweets and clicks manifold.

Curate great content out there.

One really good way to provide value to your followers is to share some rather stellar content that is provided by other people – especially those that have a large following.

Make a professional profile.

You have to pay attention towards creating a really goof profile that stands out amongst others, Make sure it is as professional as can be, complete with display picture and cover image as well.

Retweet the content of your followers.

When you get a retweet from someone, it's a really good idea to thank him or her for that retweet. You might even want to pay it back by retweeting something they might have tweeted, either at the current moment or sometime in the near future.

Don't tweet only business.

It will help to tweet things that are not related top your business every now and then. That will ensure that the people who are following you, continue to do so and don't get the feeling of being constantly spammed by tweets that promote your business.

Make sure that you follow the right people.

You need to follow the people who are actually interested in what you have to say. In order to achieve this you need to use tools like *Twellow*, which will help you identify the people in your region who are interested in the niche your product represents.

Make sure you favorite your followers' content.

Another way to show appreciation for your followers is to favorite their content; make sure you don't auto-favorite as you might be suspended by Twitter in the future for over favoring content.

Chapter 3: Instagram

Instagram is a great way to promote your business as it involves a good use of pictures that are becoming increasingly favored by people out there where it comes to getting information on the worldwide web. Let's take a look at the lowdown on Instagram marketing!

Strategies to leverage your brand worth on Instagram

Make sure you shoot *square* photographs.

This will help you ensure that nothing important is cropped out of your picture when you upload it on Instagram. Most digital cameras and smartphones have this (the taking of square photographs) as an inbuilt feature.

Create an actionable hashtag. You need to get people out there to actually interact with your brand by creating a hashtag that actually implores them to take some action. For instance, the Nike campaign *#chooseyourwinter* was one such campaign that worked wonders, and helped many connect with the brand.

Take better pictures on your smartphone. Chances that you will be using that smartphone a lot to take some stellar pictures are high, and you could simply take some online tips from sites like PopPhoto to take better pictures, rather than have to opt for a DSLR camera.

Cross-promote your partners on Instagram. You need to promote your partners as much as you possibly can. This means tagging them or simply outright professing your admiration for them. This will only lead them to promote you as well, thus helping you to get increased followers and sales in the process.

Partner with a good cause. If you partner with a good cause like an environmentally friendly one or perhaps one that is involved in the aid of the poor, you will be sending a strong message out there to the community at large, when you share that partnership on Instagram.

Post 'behind-the-scenes' pictures'. You don't wish to be constantly posting professionally shot pictures of your products/business activities. You need to get a little less personal at times. For instance, you might display candid pictures from behind the scenes of an advertisement you are shooting for your brand.

Make sure you capitalize on trending hashtags. When you see certain hashtags trending, you might wish to incorporate them into your posts in order to get them all the more visibility. You need to ensure, though, that those hashtags are relevant to your brand before you get them onboard.

Chapter 4: LinkedIn

What better way to promote your brand other than by using the most professional social media-marketing platform out there, LinkedIn? Here's a look at how to get the most out of it!

Strategies to leverage your brand worth on LinkedIn

Make sure you position yourself as an expert.

What better place to be considered an expert on your trade other than LinkedIn? You can manage to do this by constantly generating good content that serves to educate the hungry seeking minds out there, giving them the belief that you are a force to reckon with in the industry.

Create an emotional connect with your followers.

Even though this is not Facebook, it will help you to create a strong emotional bond with your followers. You need to find the people who connect with you the most, and then reach out to them to take that relationship further.

Make sure you complete that profile of yours.

One of the biggest mistakes people make is to not complete their profile. You need to ensure that you fill in all the details regarding your product or service and even your work experience, so when people see it they are enticed to get to know more about you.

Join and connect with related groups.

The best way to get to know more about the happenings in your niche industry and thus benefit from the same is to join relevant groups within your industry and indulge in the conversations posted in them. Make sure that you post threads of your own, so that you get all the more noticed. Of course you want to post something most thought provoking and one that stimulates healthy discussion. Make sure that you listen carefully to what others have to say – you might just learn a great deal in the process!

Use the Professional Portfolio feature.

You want to add plenty of videos and photos to the content you post on LinkedIn and you need to use the Professional Portfolio feature to do exactly that. It will help make your content stand out in a great way!

Make sure that you recommend others out there.

You will find that there are plenty of people out there that you can recommend, and that's exactly what you should do without them even asking you – it will only lead to them helping you back in future.

Connect directly with new people via InMail.

You need to form a great relationship with your new connections right in the very beginning, and the best way to do that is by connecting with them via InMail and sharing with them helpful articles related to your industry.

Tag your best connections in your important posts.

You will come to see that you can get all your best connections to never miss the important things you are saying, by simply tagging them in your posts. Of course you want to only tag them in important posts and not all the time.

Chapter 5: YouTube

A lot of people today are moving more towards this medium to get information on brands, and you could do well to establish a strong brand presence on this platform. Let's take a look at exactly how!

Strategies to leverage your brand worth on YouTube

Create compelling content.

Nobody is going to waste their time watching a drab video so you should ensure that rather than creating too many mundane videos, focus instead on creating only a few captivating ones that really serve to educate and perhaps even address a gap in the needs of your potential customers.

Tell a story.

Rather than being too technical in your videos, try and tell a story, as is the case with many commercial ads out there on television. When you tell a story, it really drives the engagement of people out there like nothing else.

Partner with the big guns on YouTube.

There are many people out there on YouTube who have loads of followers and it would be in the best of your interests to partner with them so that you get them to talk about you in their videos and thus increase your following in the process. Of course you have to get them to promote you first, and that can be done by offering them things like freebies – a really small price to pay, where it comes to getting loads of exposure in return.

Create Playlists of your best content.

Over time you might have created quite a few videos, but for the sake of new followers you need to ensure that you create video playlists of the very best content you have created. That will ensure that all the newcomers to your page will get only the very best first impression!

Use the AdWords Display planner to find the right keywords.

You need to use the right keywords to include when you are in the process of posting those videos, so that people out there who are really looking for your product, actually get the chance to find it.

Link people back to your website.

You might have created a rather compelling video, but what's the use if you don't drive people back to that website of yours in order to boost sales? Make sure you include a link at the end of your video, to do exactly that.

Use those YouTube ads.

You can use YouTube ads to get all the exposure that you want, by simply bidding on the keywords that people are using when they are searching for content that is related to your product or service on YouTube. It's much cheaper than a Google or Facebook ad!

Make sure your page is well optimized.

You want to optimize that page of yours, because that is what will stand out first when a customer lands there. It should have all the pertinent information on your company as well as links to your website and social media profiles.

Chapter 6: Google+

Google + is certainly not a social media platform to be left far behind, where it comes to the effective marketing of your product. Let's take a look at how we can make the most out of it.

Strategies to leverage your brand worth on Google +

Make great charts and share them.

A lot of people share inspirational images and animated gifs but when it comes to conveying some rather great statistical information, it would serve you best to create some good charts with charting software, to create a unique impact!

Fill in all the details on your profile page.

A lot of people don't take Google+ all that seriously and don't fill in all their details on their Google+ page. Make sure you do, and don't forget to include some rather catchy photographs that serve well to depict your brand in the right manner.

Use *tall* images for the best results.

You want great images to captivate the minds of people and get those click through rates higher, but that's not all; you need to ensure that the images are tall so that they take up a lot of space on the walls of your potential customers. That's a great way of getting far more visibility on the platform as opposed to other people out there who are using small images. Of course you should make sure you write some compelling content to go with that picture.

Use Google Plus Ripples to find who is sharing your content.

Unlike other social media marketing sites, you can't really find out who is sharing your content if they haven't mad e a mention of you while doing so. That's where Google Plus Ripples steps in – you can use it to find out exactly who has shared your content, and in the process connect with them.

Use the Google+ search to your advantage.

You want to see who is talking about your brand out there or perhaps even about some pertinent information that is related to the industry you are in, and the best possible way to do that is by using the Google+ search to find out exactly that. Whenever you find a relevant thread, make sure you repost it apart from commenting on the same. The key here is interaction – you have to ensure you do that well!

Use those Google+ hangouts.

One of the most interesting things on Google+ is the hangouts that you can use to get your consumers to hang out with perhaps you, or other people who are working at your business place. It's a really cool way to get a bunch of people who are all interested in the same thing, to get to connect with one another. This *hangout* feature is something that best differentiates Google+ from the other social media sites out there, so make sure you use it well to your advantage and keep your audience engaged!

Chapter 7: Pinterest

Pinterest is a great way to garner a good deal of interest in that brand of yours. Let's take a look at the lowdown on this upcoming social media-marketing platform.

Strategies to leverage your brand worth on Pinterest

Put those price tags in the pins you create.

You want to put a price tag along with the pin that you either create or repost, because the ultimate goal is to get sales and the best possible way to do that is to simply make the price of your product visible to all in the online realm.

Make those descriptions count.

You have a maximum of 500 characters for that description of your product on Pinterest, but of course you don't want to use all of them and end up creating a rather lengthy description. Make sure you at least stick to around 250 characters, though. Also, in the description you are writing you need to ensure that you include all the relevant keywords and that you possibly can, and a couple of hashtags as well, so that you ensure that your pin is actually noticed out there by people who are looking for products like yours on search engines out there.

Start curating content.

You simply have to look for some rather stellar content out there that you can repin so that the awareness of your own account increases in the process. While you want to look for items related to your industry, it's not a bad idea to post unrelated content that has been repinned many times, as well, and that is aesthetically most appealing.

Use PinGroupie to find popular group boards.

You need to find popular group boards out there so that you can take the awareness of your brand several notches higher, and using PinGroupie is a good way to do just that. Select he category that you want to see the group boards and then the order (you might wish to consider *repins* here), in order to find the groups that best fit your sensibilities.

Create a call to action to get people to subscribe.

The end goal is getting people to subscribe to that email list of yours, and creating a call to action by asking people to click in their email details in your pin can be a way to do just that. Offer them an incentive, to make it easier for them to sign up!

Chapter 8: Quora

Quora is becoming increasingly popular where it comes to promoting your brand online. Let's take a look at what it takes to be effective on this platform.

Strategies to leverage your brand worth on Quora

Ask the right questions as well.

It's not enough to simply feel that you know it all out there by answering questions posted on this unique platform. You have to ensure that you ask pertinent questions on this platform because here you will undoubtedly find great answers that you might in all probability not have come up with yourself, and that will only help take your business forward.

Answer quickly.

When you are answering a question out there, make sure you do it quick. That will ensure that you get engagement and perhaps even an upvote from the person who has asked the question, because it is still fresh in their mind.

Connect with journalists.

You really do wish to try and get some free PR out there, and Quora is a great place to find them simply because those journalists tend to come there to get valuable opinions for their stories.

Don't promote your product in those answers.

You really do not wish to promote your product in those answers of yours, simply because you are strictly seeking to add value to people by answering their questions and people will see through your ploy to market yourself in that manner. If you really do add value by answering their questions in a way that actually serves to help them, they will themselves go to your profile and find out all the information that they need where it comes to your company and the product you are selling.

Make sure that you edit and format well.

You do not wish to create a bad impression out there by providing answers that are not properly edited, and neither do you want to miss out on formatting your answers in a rather stellar way using Quora's text editing tools, so that they stand out with neatly bulleted lists and italicized and bold titles and sub titles.

Answer questions in your niche to be considered an expert.

Of course you want to be touted as the expert in your field and the best possible way to do that is by answering questions in your own field, so that you become something of an authoritative voice for people who are looking to have their needs addressed in the niche you are working in. That will only serve to make them want to buy your product more than ever.

Chapter 9: Some additional stellar tips for social media marketing

Now that we have seen all the best possible strategies where it comes to each of the most popular social media marketing platforms out there that you can use to take your brand to great horizons, it's time to take a look at some really great additional tips, that will ensure that your brand gets all the recognition it deserves out there.

Some stellar tips for that social media marketing

When in a crisis, remain calm.

You might have inadvertently said something out there that you might come to regret in hindsight; something that might draw a great deal of criticism from your target audience. In a situation like this, it's best to remain as calm as you possibly can and not say something else that will fuel the crisis even more. Stay as calm as you possibly can. However, that doesn't mean that you ignore the problem; make sure you apologize for your words that might have hurt the sentiments of many.

Be as original as you possibly can.

It's perfectly alright as a part of your strategy, to retweet that great bit of news or perhaps repin that pin out there, but for the most part you should really be looking at creating content that is fresh and original. You have to show your audience out there that you are indeed most different from the others in the online space, and showcasing your original work is the best possible way to do that!

Consider hiring a social media manager.

This is really important, especially when it comes to the long run. You might have got the initial share of likes for that Facebook page of yours, but if you really want to take it to the next level then you have to consider hiring a social media manager, who is an expert in doing exactly that. Come to think of it, you really will not have either the time or the expertise to manage your social media platforms as they grow over time, and it's best to leave the job to a professional.

Don't let everyone from your company represent your brand online.

While this is not meant to slight any of your employees (considering the fact that they too have a voice of their own that they would like to express), it's really not such a great idea to let all of them post their opinions on your social media sites. Leave it to the people who are upper crust management; in that way it's kept professional – just like it should be. The last thing you want is your employee posting things that are really not relevant to your business.

Do not delete any negative comments out there.

There will be people who are not satisfied by either your product or your service who will make it a point to vent their frustrations on your social media platforms so that your company gets duly affected in the process. The last thing you want to do is to delete a venomous comment. Instead, you could very well use this as an opportunity to talk to the customer and find out what went wrong with their experience. You never know, you might just make them happy in the process and you will be showing one and all that you truly care about the satisfaction of your customers.

Drop a few networks if they are not working for you.

The most important thing to remember when you are working on a social media marketing campaign, is the fact that you are striving hard to seek the highest engagement from your potential customers out there, and if you find that a few networks like Pinterest or Google+ are not working for you, it would not be worth your while to invest all your time and energy in them. Instead focus on the ones that are working best for you, and make sure you capitalize on them in order to produce the best possible results that will make your brand grow in a way like no other.

Examine your voice across platforms to ensure that is different for each networking site.

We have already seen the strategies that we have carved out for each of the individual social media platforms out there, but it's important that you have a different *voice* or overall essence of presenting information, for each platform. There's a reason that Facebook is Facebook and not Linkedin; make sure that your voice is intrinsically different where it comes to different platforms – because the audience for the different platforms is inherently different as well. Even if a person is using both Facebook and Linkedin, he will want to see information presented differently across both the platforms he uses.

Tailor content based on what your customers want to hear.

It's pretty easy, when you are in the process of creating great content out there, to completely forget about the needs of your customers. You have to research them and find out exactly what it is they want to hear, and then tailor content around their needs. It's very simple to get lost in the web of thinking that you have created something close to your heart and that everyone out there will like it as well. No, you have to think about others and not you!

Conclusion

Thank you again for purchasing this book!

We have seen in this book, all the best possible ways we can leverage our presence on the social media platforms out there, in order to maximize the profits we can earn where it comes to those businesses we run.

We have taken a look at the best possible social media marketing platforms in today's world, and seen the individual strategies that are associated with each of these social networking platforms, to take them to the next level.

We have also seen all the additional tips that we would need to ensure that that social media management plan is as foolproof as can possibly be. We have come to see that all of the social media platforms might not be right for us, and that we can take our pick where it comes to choosing from these most stellar platforms, so that we are ensuring that we optimize our efforts and get the best results possible out of our social media marketing campaign.

The world today is filled with people who are jumping onto the social media bandwagon every second and it would be worth your while to not waste any time and get on it as soon as possible, so that you get faster results than you could ever possibly imagine.

So, are you ready to take that social media experience of yours to the next level? Make sure that you implement all the strategies incorporated in this book where it comes to each of the social media platforms, and work your way towards the success you erstwhile only dreamed of.

Thank you and good luck!